Bouncing Belu
The Bubbly Boy

Written By Ms. Gladys
Illustrated by Daniel Aiers

"Bouncing Belu. The Bubbly Boy" by Ms. Gladys

www.pichron.com

Copyright © 2021 Ms. Gladys (first published as Gladys O.)

For permissions, please contact via:

www.pichron.com/contact

Paperback ISBN: 978-1-7778843-0-7

E-book ISBN: 978-1-7778843-1-4

DEDICATION

This book is dedicated to Tess.
The Spirit spoke through you, and I obeyed.

This Book Belongs To:

_____

Meet Bouncing Belu,
the bubbly four-year-old boy.

Bouncing Belu loves to bounce.

Bouncing Belu bounces
both day and night.

Bouncing Belu lives in a big house with his dad, mom, and big brother Bili.

Bouncing Belu and his big brother Bili have a brown puppy named Bunny.

Bouncing Belu's house has a big backyard where he and big brother Bili love to bounce around.

As they played in their backyard, Bouncing Belu's dad reminded the family that in three days, they would go to the beach house.

Bouncing Belu and big brother Bili were very happy they were going to the beach house. They began to bounce their basketball!

9

Later that night, Bouncing Belu's dad came to his room to read to him.

Bouncing Belu asked his dad again when they were going to the beach house.

His dad let him know that he had three more sleeps to go.

Bouncing Belu was so glad to hear that he had "three more sleeps to go!"

After reading to him, Bouncing Belu's dad kissed him goodnight and tucked him into bed.

11

The next day, Bouncing Belu bounced to where his dad was watering the plants.

Bouncing Belu asked his dad if it was time to go to the beach house.

Bouncing Belu's dad reminded him that he had two more sleeps to go.

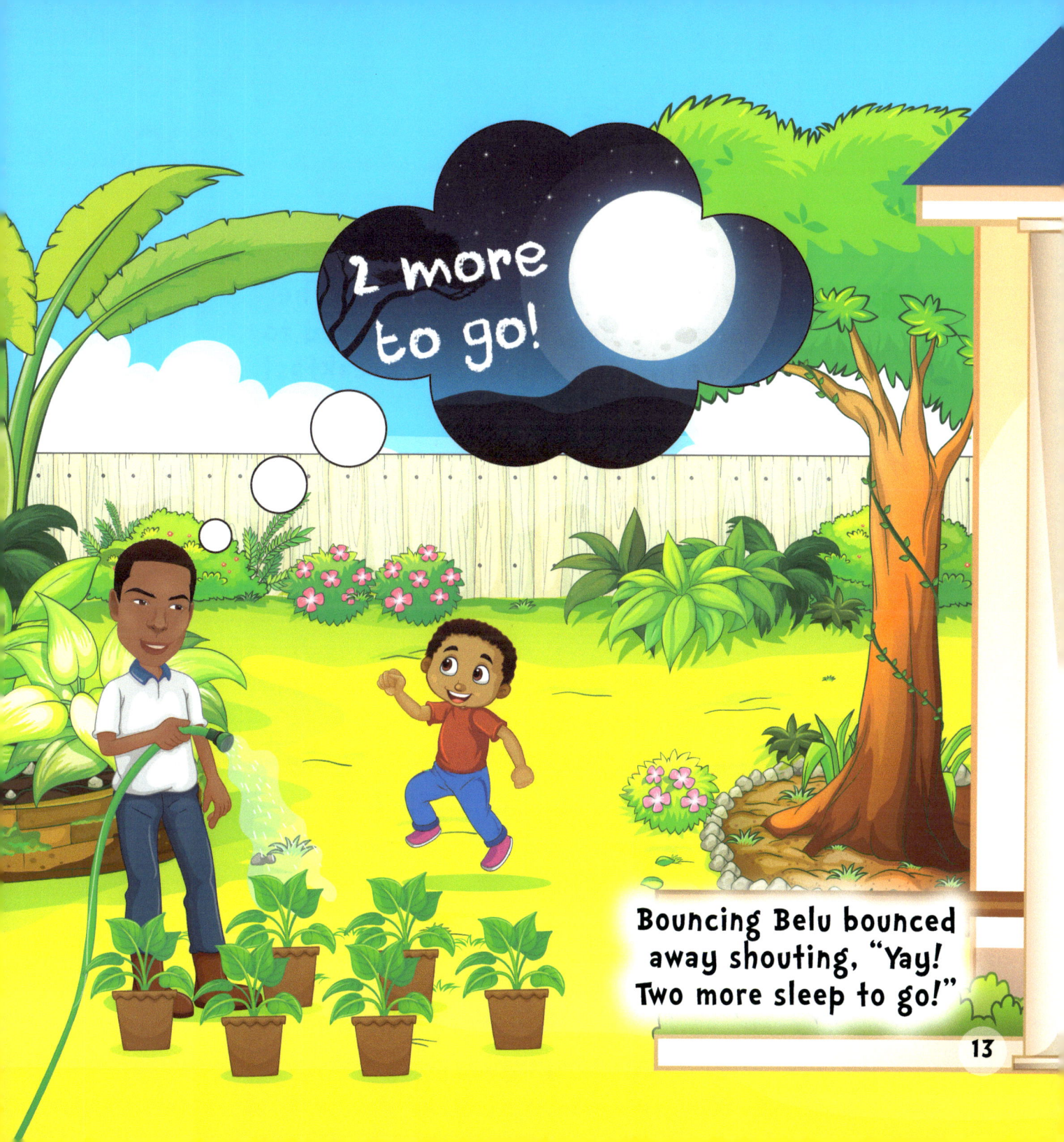

2 more to go!

Bouncing Belu bounced away shouting, "Yay! Two more sleep to go!"

13

When Bouncing Belu woke up the following day, he again bounced to where his dad was having breakfast.

Bouncing Belu asked his dad again if it was time to go to the beach house.

His dad gently reminded him that he had one more sleep to go.

1 more to go!

Bouncing Belu could not hold back his happiness!

He cheered and bounced around, saying, "Yay! One more sleep to go!"

At bedtime, Bouncing Belu and his dad
sat to read another bedtime story.

Bouncing Belu's dad read from one of
Bouncing Belu's favorite board books.

Bouncing Belu listened as his dad read to him.
He always enjoyed reading time with his dad.

While his dad was still reading, this time, it was Bouncing Belu who reminded his dad that he had one more sleep to go!

His dad laughed and continued reading.

On the day of the road trip, Bouncing Belu
bounced out of bed before everyone!

He went to his big brother Bili's bedroom,
then bounced on Bili's bed.

Big brother Bili was not bothered.
He knew why his baby brother was excited!

They both played and bounced around.
Even Bunny joined in the fun!

Bouncing Belu's mom and dad heard them.

They knew the boys were rejoicing
because it was "beach house day!"

Their mom got them ready, while their dad
loaded the car with their beach items.

After getting ready, the whole family sat down to eat breakfast.

Bouncing Belu asked his dad if he had packed their beach ball and his blue boat.

His dad smiled and said yes.

Bouncing Belu and his big brother Bili laughed out loud because they were both filled with bubbly joy!

After breakfast, Bouncing Belu, big brother Bili, and their puppy Bunny bounced all the way to the car.

Their mom and dad helped them sit in the car.

And then...

Beep!!! Beep!!! Off to the beach house they went!"

The End!

DOT-TO-DOT
AND
COLORING ACTIVITIES

Bouncing Belu reads

Bunny the puppy

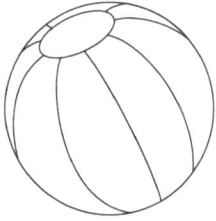

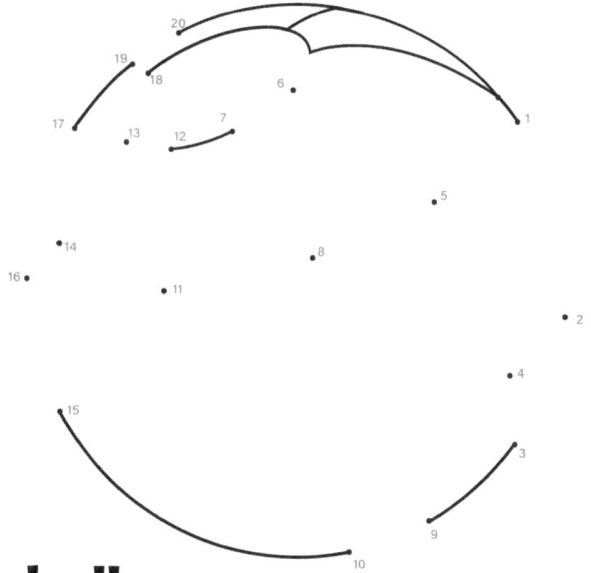

beach ball

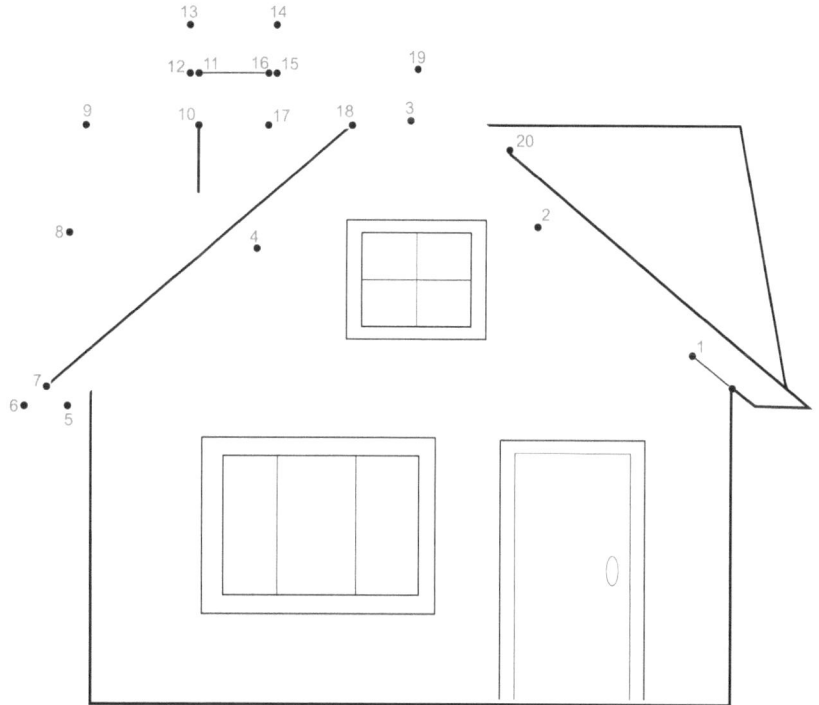

beach house

29

boat

beach bucket